This 1997 Cu...
Annual be...

Name.......................................

Age.............

I am a member of the.........................

.... Cub Scout Pack

My Cub Scout Promise
I promise that I will do my best
to do my duty to God and to the Queen,
to help other people
and to keep the Cub Scout Law.

£5.75
UK only

Contents

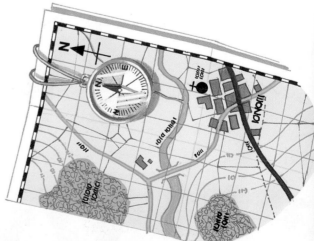

Safety Notice
Please note that the activities described in this book are suitable for children to carry out unaided. However, if adult help or supervision is thought necessary, then this has been indicated in the text and/or illustrations.

Text: Sara Fielding Illustrations: Rob Sharpe

The Chocolate Factory

Have you read the book 'Charlie and the Chocolate Factory' by Roald Dahl? Imagine being Charlie in Willy Wonka's Chocolate Factory, where you could eat as much chocolate as you wanted!

William, Darren, Ryan and Oliver of the 7th Windsor (Old Windsor) 'Baden' Cub Scout Pack had a treat when they went on a special tour of the Mars® factory in Slough, Berkshire.

They were met by Pete Gibbs. The Cubs had lots of questions to ask.

Everyone in the factory has to wear hairnets, hard hats and smart white overalls with extra large pockets – even the Cubs.

"Why are the pockets so big?" asked Ryan.

"You'll soon find out," said Pete.

Bill Thompson appeared to give the Cubs a guided tour. "How many Mars® bars do you think we make here each day?" he asked.

"Fifty?" said William.

"One hundred?" suggested Darren.

2. Warm, fresh chocolate is bendy and sticky!

The boys were given ear plugs, as the factory was very noisy, and were taken to one of the many machines. There are different machines for each brand made by Mars®. The Cubs started off by looking at the Bounty® machine. Rows and rows of white coconut lumps passed through moulds and under a small chocolate waterfall.

1. Ryan puts on a white coat and hard hat.

"Around three MILLION Mars® bars are made here each day," said Bill.

"Do you think there will be any spare for us to try?" asked William.

3. What does a one-minute-old Galaxy® bar taste like?

Text and photographs: Dave Wood

William wondered what was going to happen to some Bounties® whose wrappers were not on properly. "Help yourselves!" said Bill. The boys began to realise why the pockets on their white coats were so big!

4. Time to start filling up those pockets!

On the Topic® line a layer of chocolate had a layer of toffee spread on to it. Then came a layer of Mars' secret recipe hazelnut nougat. Bill let the boys try some!

5. Some of the 3 million Mars® bars made every day!

The boys could not believe their eyes when they saw the Mars® line. Thousands of chocolate bars filled conveyor belts which wrapped their way around the factory. Lots of bars found their way into the Cubs' pockets, thanks to Bill!

At the end of the tour, the boys thanked Bill and Pete. They staggered out of the building weighed down by the chocolates they had been given. Some even made it back to the Pack to share with the other Cubs!

6. If only it were real!

Thanks to Pete Gibbs, Bill Thompson and all at Mars Confectionery, Slough, for their help. Please note that private visits for groups of Cub Scouts are not available.

Have Fun with Maths!

Magic 7

Amaze a friend! Ask him to write down a 3-figure number. Then tell him to…

Times the number by 2.
Add 5.
Subtract 3.
Add 12.
Divide by 2.
Subtract the number first thought of.

Stun your friend by telling him that the answer is 7! How do you know? Try this with any number. The answer is always the same!

123
×2
=246
+5
=251
−3
=248
+12
=260
÷2
=130
−123
=7

Sequences

Fill in the missing numbers.

1. **7   10   13   ?   19**

2. **5   7   10   ?   19**

3. **80   70   61   ?   46**

4. **1   16   2   15   3   ?   4   13**

Number puzzle one

Across
3. 369 + 262 =
5. 823 − 15 =
7. 11 + 11 =

Down
1. 148 − 92 =
2. 39 + 71 =
4. 159 + 223 =
6. 72 + 12 =

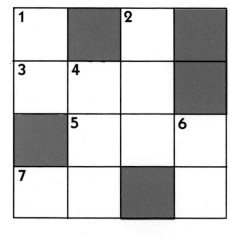

Can you help?

1. Tom has eaten half of the bag of 30 sweets his gran bought him. He eats six more before his mum tells him to stop. How many sweets has Tom eaten altogether?

2. Akela has a Cub Scout Pack of 19 boys and girls. There are five in Blue Six, five in White Six and five in Red Six. How many Cub Scouts in Yellow Six?

Text: Karen Hankey Illustrations: Mike Turner

Magic squares

Each row in this square adds up to the same number, across, down and diagonally. Can you work out the missing numbers?

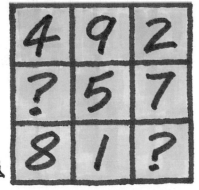

4	9	2
?	5	7
8	1	?

And this one?

7	12	?	14
2	13	8	?
16	3	10	5
?	6	15	4

Buzz, fizz

A game to play with friends. Stand in a circle. Start counting around the circle from number one. When someone gets to a number that can be **divided by three**, they must shout 'buzz'. For example, one, two, buzz, four, five, buzz and so on.

Play with numbers that can be divided by four, but this time, shout 'fizz'.

Can you play 'buzz' **and** 'fizz'? Start off one, two, buzz, fizz, five, buzz and so on.

Number puzzle two

Across
1. 275 − 60 =
2. 36 + 22 =
3. 58 + 74 =
5. 100 − 50 =

Down
1. 147 + 136 =
2. 608 − 92 =
4. 36 − 11 =

Answers are on page 63.

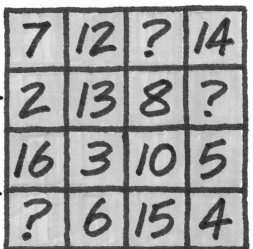

Chocolate Pastries

**Make some Chocolate Pastries for your family or friends.
They're so yummy I bet you'll eat most of them yourself!**

You will need
• a small block of puff pastry (ready-made from supermarkets). If it is frozen, defrost it
• chocolate spread   • icing sugar   • flour

Before you begin…
• Wash your hands.
• Put on an apron.
• Ask an adult to preheat the oven to gas mark 7/ 220°C/425°F.
• Collect all the things you need.

1 Sprinkle a little flour on a work surface. Put some flour on a rolling pin too. This stops the pastry sticking.

2 Roll the pastry out evenly so that it is quite thin. It should be a bit thicker than the cover of this Annual. You may need an adult to help.

Recipe: Emma Wood   Illustrations: Wendy Hesse

3 Brush any loose flour off the pastry. Spread the chocolate over the top.

4 Fold the pastry in half. Cut it into slices about 1 to 2 cm wide.

5 Sprinkle a little flour on a baking tray. Put the slices on the tray. Bake near the top of the oven for 10 to 15 minutes.

6 Ask an adult to take the pastries out of the oven. Cool. Put them on a wire rack. Sprinkle with icing sugar. Leave to cool.

Roller Blade Rescue!

Blue Six were ready! They were about to enter a big Cub Scout roller blading competition. They were really looking forward to it. They were all top roller bladers. Glenn had had a pair for Christmas. Now Blue Six all had skates and were totally hooked!

The six of them, Glenn, Grant, Graham, Tim and the twins, Bethanie and Jamie were waiting outside the Scout hut for Akela. He had offered to take them to the competition in the Pack minibus.

"We're going to be late!" said Bethanie, slinging her skates over her shoulder.

"It's okay," said Jamie. "Akela won't let us down."

Blue Six waited and waited, but Aklela didn't arrive. In the end they put their skates on and went over to Akela's house which was about a mile away.

On the way they were very careful. Because they were all Cub Scouts they knew they had to think about road safety and watch out for pedestrians. They soon got to Akela's house. The minibus was parked in the drive but there were no signs of life. Glenn knocked on the door, but there was no reply. Blue Six decided to look for Akela at the back of the house.

The back door was ajar and the window pane above the lock was smashed. "What if it's burglars!" said Grant.

Text: Sara Fielding Illustrations: Phil Garner

Blue Six took a look inside the house. Everything seemed to be in order.

Then, suddenly, from the far end of the garden, they heard a door banging in the wind.

Blue Six went to investigate. At the bottom of the garden was an old shed. The door was open.

Blue Six went inside. At the back of the shed was a wall of shelves. Akela was on the floor, lying next to a fallen ladder!

Glenn made a plan. "Look after Akela but don't move him," he said to the twins and Grant. "I'll phone for help."

"But, Glenn, don't you remember?" said Graham, "Akela isn't on the phone. He only moved in here a few weeks ago!"

"No problem," said Glenn bravely. "There's a farm about half a mile back down the road. I'll ring for an ambulance from there." The road outside Akela's house was very smooth, so Glenn put on his roller blades and skated there.

While he was gone, the rest of Blue Six made Akela comfortable. They tried to work out what had happened to him. As they were talking, Akela began to wake up.

"Ouch!" he said. "I think I've broken my leg!"

Akela explained what had happened. "I locked myself out of the house without the minibus keys. I had to break the glass in the door to get into the house. I came down here to get a hammer and nails to mend the door but I fell off the ladder. I'm sorry, Blue Six, I've let you all down."

"It's okay, Akela," said Jamie. "We're just glad we found you!"

At that moment they all heard a faint siren in the distance. Blue Six ran to the front of the house. There was Glenn, skating back down the road, followed by an ambulance.

Blue Six helped the crew to get Akela into the ambulance. They went with him to the hospital.

Blue Six waited at the hospital to make sure that Akela was going to be all right. They were very worried but also a bit fed up. The competition would be in full swing, without them!

As they sat gloomily in the waiting room, the ambulance crew came over to them. "We're very impressed with you Cub Scouts," they said. "Akela is going to be fine. He's in X-ray. He told us where you guys are supposed to be. We're off duty now. Do you want a lift to the competition? It might not be too late."

"YES PLEASE!" said Blue Six all at the same time!

Sirens flashing, the ambulance crew got Blue Six to the competition in record time. They were just in time to enter the freestyle competition. Guess who won? Yes, it was Glenn!

What a rescue! What a great day for Blue Six!

The Escaping Card Magic Trick

Have you ever wondered how some magic tricks are done? Well now it's your turn to be a magician and amaze your family and friends!

Some things to remember...
Magic is supposed to be fun – enjoy performing your tricks and rehearse them well before you show them to people.
Don't perform a trick more than once to the same audience and never tell anyone how it is done.

Making the trick

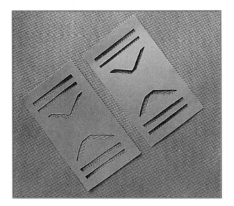

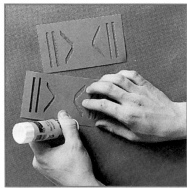

You will need
- coloured card
- paper fastener ● glue
- decoration ● scissors
- ruler ● pencils ● an adult

1 Make the cage. Trace the template on this page twice. Cut out. You may need adult help.

2 Glue along the edges as shown. Stick the two pieces together.

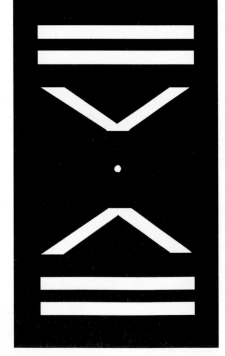

▲ Template

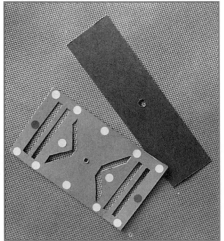

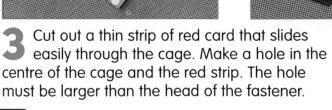

3 Cut out a thin strip of red card that slides easily through the cage. Make a hole in the centre of the cage and the red strip. The hole must be larger than the head of the fastener.

4 Put the red card into the cage. Fix in place with the fastener.

Text: Peter Barker Photographs: Dave Smith

20

Performing the trick

1 Show the audience the cage and give the red card a pull to show that it is firmly fixed. Next, remove the fastener, show it to the audience, then remove the red card.

2 Tell the audience that you will now replace the card and secure it with the fastener. Then you will make the card escape from the cage without removing the fastener!

3 With the front of the cage facing the audience, slide the card into the cage and allow it to come out at the back of the cage at the first V-shaped hole. Pass it along the back of the cage as shown, slide it back in at the bottom and replace the fastener from the back to the front. ▶

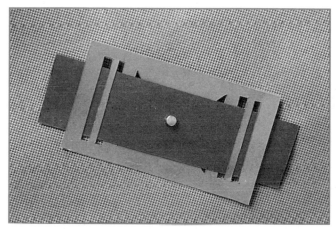

4 The trick should now look like this from the back (the side you see).

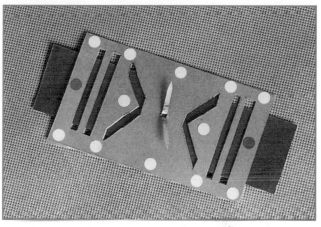

5 It should look like this from the front (the side the audience sees).

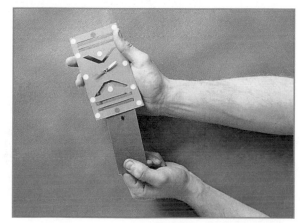

6 Say a few magic words and wiggle the red card about, allowing the hole to pass over the head of the fastener. Slip the card out of the cage, leaving the fastener in place.

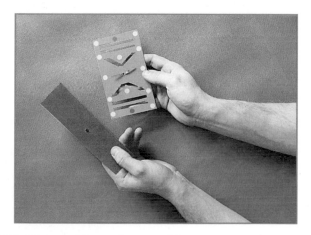

7 Hey presto – the card has escaped before their very eyes. Show the audience the cage, with the fastener still in place, and take a bow!

ROBOCUB

BY DAVE KING

CUB SCOUT RICK RICHARDS AND HIS AMAZING INVENTION, ROBOCUB, ARE WORKING IN RICK'S GARDEN SHED LABORATORY ONE MORNING, WHEN...

YEOW!

WHAT'S GOING ON?

IT FEELS LIKE A HERD OF BROWNIES MARCHING OUTSIDE! ≡BEEP!≡

RICK! YOU'VE GOT TO DO SOMETHING!

A GIANT METAL DINOSAUR IS RAMPAGING THROUGH THE PRECINCT!

BLIMEY! THIS LOOKS LIKE A JOB FOR...

...ME! HEH!

AND, ONE HURRIED TRIP TO THE SHOPPING PRECINCT LATER...

RARRGH!

THAT IS ONE SERIOUS CASE OF URBAN RENEWAL!

MAYBE HE'S UPSET BECAUSE HE COULDN'T FIND A PARKING SPACE! ≡BEEP!≡

EEK!!

OI! MY TAXES PAID FOR THAT LAMP POST!

Flea Facts

Fleas are insects. They are parasites. They feed on the blood of animals or humans. Here are 20 Flea Facts.

1 A flea can jump a hundred times its own height. Most humans cannot jump three times their own height, even with a pole.

2 Fleas can jump lengths of up to 30cm. Very large back legs help them leap.

3 Fleas move forward with a force 20 times greater than the force needed to launch a space rocket.

4 Hungry fleas may have to jump hundreds of times to land on an animal to feed on.

5 A human-sized flea could jump over a forty-storey building.

6 Fleas cut into the skin to feed on the host's blood. They have special mouth parts to pierce and suck.

7 Fleas share our homes. They bite our pets and ourselves.

8 Many fleas live on one kind of animal, like cat fleas, dog fleas, and so on.

9 The cat flea is the most common of all fleas, followed by the dog flea.

10 If a flea bites you, it will leave a red spot on your skin that will itch for a few days.

Text: Alison Davis Illustrations: Mike Turner

24

11 Fleas have claws on their legs and bristles on their bodies to help them grip to hair and skin.

12 Female fleas feed on blood before they lay eggs.

13 There are 1,800 kinds of flea in Europe, and many more throughout the world.

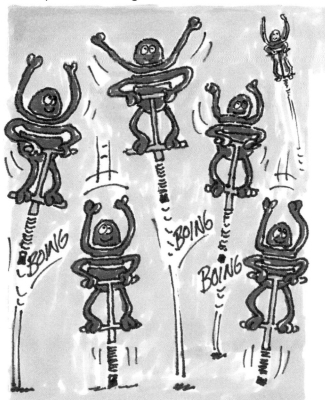

14 When they land, fleas can bounce back even faster.

15 The oriental rat flea carries bubonic plague. This disease killed millions of people in the 17th century.

16 Fleas are small insects, from 1mm to 9mm in length.

17 Fleas have very hard bodies which protect them.

18 Fleas can live for a long time without feeding.

19 Each female lays hundreds of eggs. These hatch into white worm-like larvae in ten days.

20 Fleas find new hosts by the warmth of their bodies.

A Hot Air Balloon

Ask a grown-up to help you
make this hot air balloon!

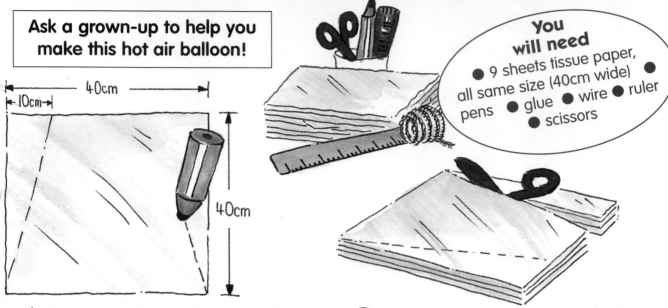

You will need
- 9 sheets tissue paper, all same size (40cm wide)
- glue ● wire ● ruler
- pens
- scissors

1 Cut out one 40cm x 40cm piece of tissue paper. Measure 10cm from one corner. Make a mark. Do the same from the other corner. Draw lines from the corners to the marks.

2 Put 3 more sheets of tissue under the one you have marked out. Cut along the lines you drew, to make 4 sheets all the same. Put the sheets to one side.

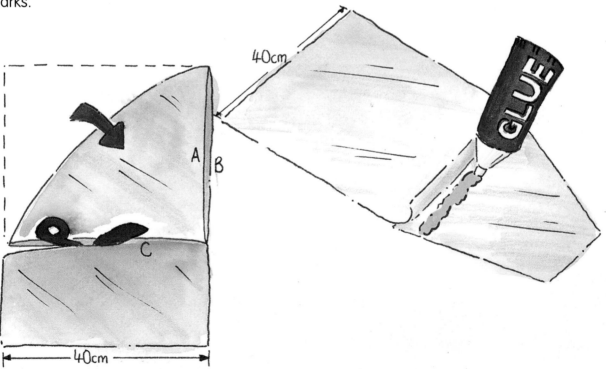

3 Take another piece of tissue 40cm wide. Fold edge **A** to edge **B**. Cut along edge **C**. You should have a square.

4 Make the balloon in 4 sections. For each section, glue a whole sheet of tissue to one of the 4 sheets you cut in step 2. Make 4.

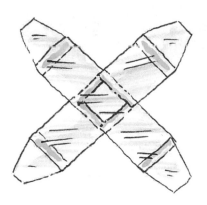

6 Fold the square. Glue along edges **D**.

5 Glue the 4 sections to the square you made in step 3.

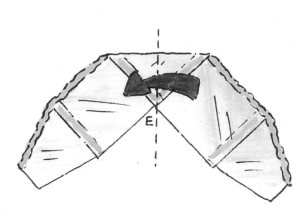

7 Lift everything up by corner **E**. Fold across the opposite diagonal. Glue the edges.

8 Make a circle of wire to fit into the mouth of the balloon. Twist glued paper around the join. Cut off any extra wire. Put the wire inside the balloon. Cut small slits around the mouth. Fold and glue over the wire, to seal into the balloon.

9 To fly your balloon, you need a hairdryer and adult help. Hold the balloon upright by the seams, with the mouth over the hairdryer. Let the adult fill the balloon with hot air. When you feel the balloon rising, let it go!

REMEMBER...
Fly on a calm day.
Check wind direction so balloon doesn't fly into trees or houses.
Do not fly within 3km of an airport.
Respect other people's property, especially farmers'!

27

Where's North?

When out and about with your Pack or finding your way with a map, you may have to find your way around. So how do you find north?

With a compass

A compass has a magnetic needle which always points from north to south. Using this, you can easily work out directions.

One of the most popular compasses is the Silva-type. The red end of the compass needle points towards north.

Hold the compass in the flat of your hand. Turn it around until the **red** end of the needle lines up over the **orienting arrow**. Once you know which way is north you will also be able to see where south, east and west are.

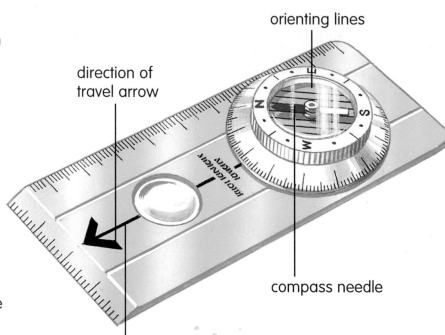

orienting lines

direction of travel arrow

compass needle

index pointer

Can you fill in the directions in between?

N

W   E

S

Text: Karen Hankey Illustrations: Clive Spong

Make your own compass

You will need
- magnet • steel needle
- shallow dish of water
- piece of cork

1 Make the needle magnetic by stroking it with the magnet about 50 times. Always move the magnet in the same direction and lift it away from the needle after each stroke.

2 Put the needle on top of the cork. Float in the dish of water. Give the needle time to settle. It will then point north and south.

Use a compass to set your map. Place the compass on the map. Turn the map around until the north arrow on the map points in the same direction as the compass needle.

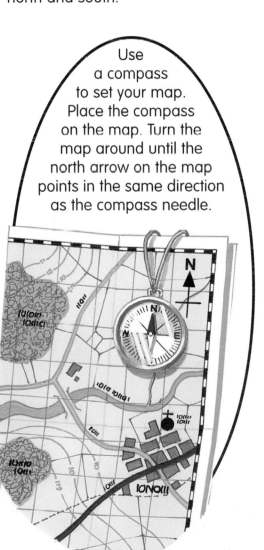

What if you are out and about without a compass?

Look at a watch. In winter, the sun is in the south at 12 noon. At 6 am it is in the east and at 6 pm it is due west.

The wind in Britain blows from the south west. Look at the smoke from tall chimneys – it will blow to the north east.

Trees in the open are affected by wind direction. They tend to lean to the north east.

On a map, find two features such as a church and a large hill. Turn the map around until the map signs point to the real things.

Look at a newly cut tree stump. The rings in the trunk are more widely spaced on the south side.

Moss tends to grow on the north side of trees or stones.

In a church, the altar is usually at the eastern end.

The Walls of History

Throughout history walls have been used as a defence against enemies and to mark boundaries. Here are some famous walls from around the world.

The Walls of Jericho

Jericho is the world's earliest town, on the border of Israel and Jordan. People have lived there for more than 11,000 years. About 10,000 years ago a huge stone wall was built around Jericho. The wall was 3m thick. When it was uncovered by archaeologists in the 1950s, one bit of the wall was still standing 8m high! Some people think the wall was built to defend the town's population from attackers, others say it was to protect Jericho from flooding. According to the Bible, this famous wall fell down when an army, led by Joshua, let out a great shout, while priests blew trumpets.

The Great Wall of China

This is the longest structure on Earth and is visible from the moon. It is 6,400km long and was built to protect China's northern border against invaders. First started in the 5th century BC, it was added to in the centuries that followed. Much of the wall was built in the 1400s and 1500s AD. A lot of the wall is in mountainous areas. Parts of it are wide enough for people to walk and cycle along. Many forts were built along it to house soldiers. It is 8m high and 4m across. It is made from bricks, stone and earth.

Text: Stephen Nixey Illustrations: Mark Stacey

Hadrian's Wall

The Romans built this great defensive wall between AD 122 and 128. It was built to protect Roman Britain from the fierce northern tribes of Picts and Scots. The wall is named after the Roman emperor Hadrian on whose orders it was built. It is 117km long and 4m high. It stretches from the Solway Firth to the mouth of the River Tyne. There are many forts, milecastles and signal turrets along it. Parts of it were painted white, so it could be seen from a distance.

Antonine Wall

In AD 142, another wall was built in Roman Britain. This wall is called the Antonine Wall because it was built during the reign of the emperor Antoninus Pius. It was built to the north of Hadrian's Wall and is only 64km long. It was made of turf on top of stone foundations.

WHAT ARE OLD WALLS MADE OF?

Wattle and daub
Some of the earliest walls are made from a network of twigs covered with thick clay.

Dry-stone walls
Look for these in the countryside. Different sized stones are packed tightly together. The stones are not stuck together, they are 'dry'.

Bricks
The first brick walls in Britain date from the 1300s. Bricks have been made in lots of different sizes. They can be put together in many different ways, making walls with interesting patterns. Every brick pattern has its own name, such as English Garden Wall bond or Flemish bond.

Don't Be Afraid to Scream!

Everyone knows that if you break the law you may end up in prison. But long ago people who broke the law were often punished in very cruel ways. At the London Dungeon you can see what horrible things happened to people who broke the law in the past. It's gruesome and scary, but we found a group of the bravest Cub Scouts, from the 1st and 4th Hanworth Cub Scout Pack, who spent a day at the dungeons.

This gruesome character is one of the guides in the dungeons.

This ugly-looking character showed the Cubs around and kept them all in order – as you can see!

Many exhibits are in cages. Paul has become part of the display!

Prisoners used to be kept in chains called shackles. Mitul, Darren and Mark tried some on.

Text: Peter Barker Photographs: Hazel Palmer and Peter Barker

32

The boys hear the story of Jack the Ripper, a notorious Victorian murderer, whose true identity remains a mystery even today.

Many years ago, people in France had their heads chopped off if they broke the law. This was done by a machine called a guillotine. Mitul tries out the Dungeon's pretend neck chopper!

The end of the tour. The Cubs have all braved the trip and enjoyed it. Why not pay the London Dungeon a visit? It's a great day out – but don't be afraid to scream!

With grateful thanks to the staff of the London Dungeon, Tooley Street, London for making this feature possible.

Mark mixes up some poisons – pretend ones!

Going to Scouts

Andrew peered into the bathroom mirror and grinned. He knew he looked good in the red scarf and green Cub Scout sweatshirt. He touched the blue woggle that held his scarf together. It felt odd to be wearing it on a Thursday. The Cubs had their Meeting on a Monday – Thursday was for Scouts.

Andrew took a deep breath as he went into the Scout Hall. He almost wished his mum was there, but she was back at the gate where he had asked her to wait.

"Hello, Andrew," said Akela and Philip. They were waiting by the door. He felt better – this wasn't so bad after all!

It was after the Meeting last week that Akela had called him over.

"You know you are old enough to join Scouts?" she said.

Andrew nodded. He was almost ten and a half.

"How would you like to go along to Scouts and see what they do?" Akela asked.

Andrew had agreed eagerly. He felt very grown up.

Andrew knew all about Scouts. The Scout Leader, Philip, often helped Akela at Cubs. Sometimes the older Scouts came too – and they knew some great games. But he was nervous. They were all so much bigger than him – and how would he know what to do?

He saw Emily, a girl who lived on his street.

"I didn't know you were a Scout," said Andrew.

"I'm Patrol Leader in Eagle Patrol," she said.

Philip explained. "That's like Sixes in Cubs, but we call our Patrols after birds."

The Meeting began. Andrew looked around. There were about twenty boys and girls. He recognised some and everyone seemed friendly. Emily guided him through inspection and flag break.

Text: Karen Hankey Illustrations: Phil Garner

The evening passed in a whirl.

Although he didn't understand everything, Andrew recognised things that he had done in Cubs.

The Scouts were going on a hike and were using maps to plan their route. Next was a game. It was one that he played in Cubs and Andrew ran around dodging the ball with the Scouts.

Later, as he waited for his mum to arrive, Andrew realised how tired he was.

Scouts is a bit like Cubs, he thought, but the Scouts do a lot more things by themselves.

Philip came over. "I thought you might like this," he said, giving Andrew a piece of paper. "It's the Scout Promise."

Andrew began to read. "On my honour, I promise that I will do my best to do my duty to God and to the Queen, to help other people and to keep the Scout Law."

Andrew said, "It's almost the same as the Cub Promise – I'll be able to remember this!"

"I'm sure you will," said Philip. "Will we see you again next week?"

"Of course!" Andrew replied. He was looking forward to finding out more about Scouts.

Names of Places

We use place-names all the time. We say, "We're going to Brighton," or, "I live in Newcastle." People thought up place-names so that other people would know exactly where they meant.

What are place-names, and where do they come from?

A place-name is the name given to a place of settlement (such as a town or a village), or to a feature in the landscape (such as a hill or a river). Many of these names are hundreds or even thousands of years old, and can be traced back to the people who used to live in Britain.

The Celts lived in Britain before the Romans came here. They spoke a language which was like the languages we now call Irish, Welsh, Gaelic and Cornish. It was the Celts who gave us the names of our greatest rivers – the Thames, Severn, Avon and Teme. They also named hills such as the Malverns, the Pennines and the Cheviots.

The Romans settled here after their invasion of AD43. They spoke Latin. Most places had already been named so all the Romans did was to make them sound a bit 'Latin'. Lincoln used to be called 'Lindo' by the Celts. The Romans changed this to 'Lindum Colonia'. Gradually, the name changed to Lincoln. Can you see how this could have happened?

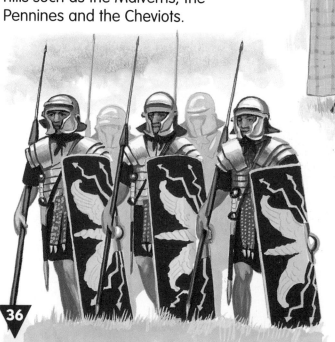

Text: Ron Crabb Illustrations: Mark Stacey

The Anglo-Saxons invaded in about AD450. Their language is called Old English. You might not think that Birmingham is a very old place – but when you know how to 'read' a place-name it's surprising to discover how old it really is. When an Anglo-Saxon called Beorma built a village, he called it 'Beormingham' ('the village of Beorma's people').

The Vikings settled here from the late 800s. They re-named some places in their language, Old Norse. Place-names that end in 'by' go back to Viking times. It means a village. Grimsby means 'Grim's village'.

The Normans invaded in 1066. They re-named some places in their language, French. Most place-names with French connections have the word 'beau' or 'bel' in them, meaning 'beautiful' or 'fine'. Places such as Beaumont, Beauchief, Belper and Belvoir were all named by French-speaking people.

How can I find out more?

Look in a dictionary of place-names in a library. To get you started, here is a list of some common parts of place-names, and what they mean. Do you know any places that have these parts in their names?

Barrow-, Bar-, -berry, -borough means the place of a hill or burial mound.

Caster-, Chester-, -caster, -cester, -chester means the place of a Roman town.

-ham means the place of a village, a manor or a homestead.

-holme means the place of a small island.

Pen- means the place of a hill.

Strat-, Stret-, Strad-, Streat-, Sturt-, -street means the place of a Roman road.

Camp Fire Yells

QUESTION: What is very warm, very noisy, takes place at Camps and Pack Holidays and is great fun?

ANSWER: A Cub Scout Camp Fire!

If you have been lucky enough to go to a Cub Camp or Pack Holiday, you might have had a Camp Fire one evening. All the Cubs, Leaders and helpers sit down together around a huge, roaring fire.

One Leader looks after the building of the fire. Another Leader is in charge of the Camp Fire itself. He or she will lead everybody in lots of singing. Camp Fire songs are usually funny, short and nearly always VERY loud! Sometimes, the Leader asks Sixes to perform short 'sketches' (three-minute-long shows).

Here is a Camp Fire sketch:

A policeman (P) stands in the acting area. He sees a rough-looking boy (B) coming towards him.
P: What's your name and what have you been doing?
B: Me name's Jake, and I've been throwing peanuts over the wall.
P: All right then, move along.
The boy leaves. Another comes along, and the same words are said, with a different name. They have all been 'throwing peanuts over the wall'. This carries on until the last person appears, with his arm in a sling, bandaged up and limping.
P: Hold on a minute – what's your name?
B: PEANUTS!

Text: Emma Wood Illustrations: Jeannette Slater

After a sketch the Leader often starts a CAMP FIRE YELL, a special way of saying 'well done' to the actors. Here is a yell:

LEADER: Give me a B.
ALL: B.
LEADER: Give me an R.
ALL: R.
LEADER: Give me an A.
ALL: A.
LEADER: Give me a V.
ALL: V.
LEADER: Give me an O.
ALL: O.
LEADER: Put them together and what have you got?
ALL: BRAVO!

Some sketches are the sort of jokes that make you groan, rather than laugh. Here's a yell to show how shocking the audience found a sketch:

ALL: One thousand volts, two thousand volts, three thousand volts, four thousand volts... SHOCKING!

For an even weaker joke yell...

ALL: Monday! Tuesday! Wednesday! Thursday! Friday! Saturday! Sunday! WEEK!

Here's a yell that Cub Scouts enjoy shouting at any time...

LEADER: Uggy uggy uggy!
ALL: Oi oi oi!
LEADER: Uggy uggy uggy!
ALL: Oi oi oi!
LEADER: Uggy!
ALL: Oi!
LEADER: Uggy!
ALL: Oi!
LEADER: Uggy uggy uggy!
ALL: Oi oi oi!

A yell called 'Ham and Eggs' needs the audience divided into two halves, 1 and 2. Each half chants the words fairly slowly.

1: Ham and eggs!
2: Ham and eggs!
1: I like mine done nice and brown!
2: I like mine turned upside down!
1: Flip 'em!
2: Flop 'em!
1: Flop 'em!
2: Flip 'em!
ALL: HAM AND EGGS!

At Camp Fires remember...
• Never throw anything on to the fire.
• Don't get too close to the fire.
• Don't talk while a Six is doing a sketch.
• Don't mess around during songs.
• HAVE FUN!

Amazing Mazes

The first mazes were called labyrinths. These puzzling networks of passages and rooms were probably built to confuse enemies. Once you went in it was very difficult to find the way out! Labyrinth designs have been found carved on rocks and painted on pottery.

Theseus in the Labyrinth

There was a famous labyrinth on the Greek island of Crete. A fierce Minotaur – half man and half bull – lived in it. No one who went in ever came out again. Every year the king, Minos, sent fourteen boys and girls into the labyrinth for the Minotaur to eat.

Theseus said he would go into the labyrinth to kill the Minotaur. He took a sword and a ball of thread with him. He tied one end of the thread to the door and set off.

Theseus went this way and that through the maze of dark passages. At last he found the Minotaur. After a long fight, he killed it.

How did Theseus find his way out? He followed the thread. It led him back the way he had come. Soon he was free!

Mazes Old and New

Mazes made with plants were built in gardens.

The maze at Hampton Court, near London, was made in 1690. You can still go round it today.

The longest maze in the world was built in 1978 at Longleat House, Wiltshire. It is 2.4 kilometres long and made of 16,180 yew trees.

Text: Alison Davis Illustrations: Peter Stevenson

Try to find your way through these mazes!

Help this hungry mouse find his dinner.

Show the Cub Scout the way to the camp site.

Help the mummy find the way back to his tomb in the pyramid.

The Prancing Horse is 50!

1997 marks the 50th birthday of the most famous sports car maker in the world – the Italian firm of Ferrari. It was started by Enzo Ferrari and soon became famous for its successes in international car racing. Since then, Ferraris have been regulars in autosport, with Michael Schumacher from Germany the team's star driver.

It's not only on the racing track that Ferrari has been successful. The company has made road-going sports cars too. For Ferrari's 40th birthday, the F40 was produced. It was the first road-going car that could go faster than 200 mph (322 km/h). For Ferrari's 50th birthday, the F50 has been made – a Formula One track racer that can be driven on the roads. Whether it can be driven in safety without proper training is another matter! You need more than pocket-money if you want an F50 though – in the UK it sells for a whopping £329,000!

BLOOD RED

Red is the official colour of car-mad Italy's racing cars, and almost all Ferraris come in that colour too. You can buy Ferraris in other colours, but almost nobody does! Even the engines often have red parts – in fact, the Ferrari Testarossa is named after the Italian words 'red head', for the engine bits painted in that colour!

WHY THE PRANCING HORSE?

Enzo Ferrari took the black prancing horse of a World War I Italian flying ace, Francesco Baracca, as the symbol of his car firm. It was a mark of respect for Baracca's skills in the air.

Every Ferrari wears the black and yellow prancing horse badge.

Text and photographs: David Jefferis

FERRARIS IN MINIATURE

Real Ferraris are mighty expensive – even the cheapest F355 Berlinetta costs nearly £90,000. So, not surprisingly, models are more popular with Ferrari enthusiasts. Models come in lots of scales and sizes. The four models shown here range from the tiny 1:60 scale Testarossa to the 1:43 scale F40 to the larger 1:24 F40 and giant-size 1:18 scale F50. Even though they are thought of as 'toys', miniatures like these are made very precisely, and a big model is made up of dozens of parts.

Ferrari interiors are workmanlike affairs, with few luxuries.

Fins, wings and air intakes are typical trademarks of modern Ferrari cars.

Smooth streamlined looks mark out Ferraris. Shapes like this slip more easily through the air than square, upright ones.

Early Ferrari racers had skinny tyres and upright radiators.

AHJ 76C

Simple First Aid

Imagine you are out playing with your friends when one of them falls over and cuts his knee. Would you know what to do?

Learn some simple first aid skills to help you cope with common accidents. You won't become a first aider by reading this so learn some more about it before dealing with other incidents. Ask an **adult** to read this article with you. Practise these skills with him or her so that you know how to cope in the event of the real thing happening. Why not ask Akela if you can learn more first aid as a whole Cub Scout Pack? If you are ever faced with a bigger problem, always get help. If someone has been badly hurt or injured, get adult help. An ambulance or doctor should be called right away.

Minor cuts

If someone has a small cut (one that is not pouring with blood!), wash your hands before dealing with the wound. If you can find some protective gloves, put them on before doing any first aid to protect you and the casualty. If the cut is dirty, rinse it with running water until it is clean.

Carefully clean the surrounding area with soap and water, gently wiping away from the edges of the wound. If bleeding does not stop, raise the injured part and gently apply pressure to the wound. Cover with a dressing.

If in doubt about the injury, seek medical advice.

What is first aid?
First aid is the first treatment given to a person who has been hurt or become ill. If you're the first person on hand when someone is hurt, it could be up to you to give any first aid needed.

Text: Peter Barker Illustrations: Linda Worrall

Burns and scalds

Burns and scalds can be very painful and require cooling as quickly as possible. Reassure the casualty and place the injured part under running cold water or immerse it in cold water for at least 10 minutes – longer if it still hurts. Remove any rings, watches, belts, shoes or any other items before the area starts to swell. Dress the area with a clean, sterile dressing.

Do not apply any creams to the area or use plasters or sticky dressings. If the area blisters, do not pop it or try to remove any loose skin.

Fainting

Fainting happens when the flow of blood to the brain is reduced for a brief moment. This can be because of a nervous reaction or as the result of exhaustion or lack of food.

If someone feels faint, or has fainted, lay him down on his back and raise his legs into the air with a pillow, blanket or something similar. Lift his chin to ensure that his airway is kept open.

Loosen any tight clothing at the neck, chest and waist to help his breathing and circulation. Make sure he has plenty of fresh air. When he starts to come around, reassure him and slowly help him into a sitting position.

Creature Quiz

If you go down to the woods today...

...don't just look up and around at the trees and bushes. Instead, look down at the ground you're walking on, especially if it's a footpath covered in thick mud or snow. You never know what secrets paths may reveal!

As animals move around they, like us, leave footprints behind. Some animals leave big, heavy prints. Others leave small, soft prints. Footprints are good clues to which animals are around. With a bit of practice you can learn to recognise animal footprints. Your local library will have useful books.

To get you started on your detective work, can you match these sets of footprints to the animals who made them?

Answers are on page 63.

a. hedgehog

b. otter

1

2

3

c. grey squirrel

d. fox

e. badger

f. fallow deer

An Origami House

Origami has been a popular art in Japan for about 1,000 years. In origami paper is folded to make animals, figures – and a house like this one!

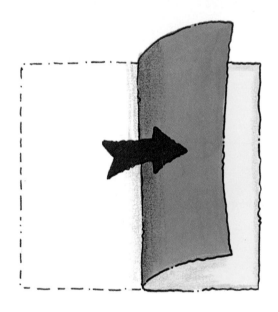

1 Lay the paper flat. Fold in half from side to side. Unfold.

2 Fold the top corners down to meet the fold-line you made in step 1.

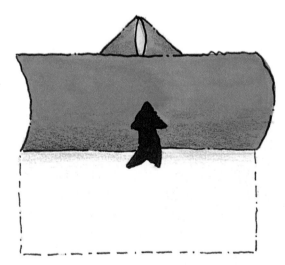

3 Fold the bottom half of the paper up. It should cover the triangle.

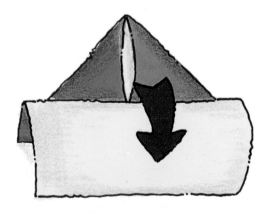

4 Fold the top layer of paper down. It should make a small pleat.

Text: Ron Crabb Illustrations: Jeannette Slater

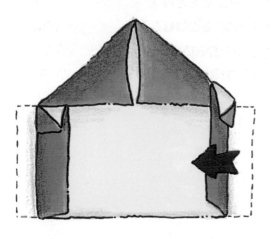

5 Fold the left and right sides of the base in.

6 Press on the top of the side folds to make triangles.

7 Turn the paper over to see your paper-fold house.

Why not paint a door and windows on your house? Or cut out a paper door and windows and glue them in place. What else could you add to your origami house?

A Ship Called 'Matthew'

Five hundred years ago, an explorer sailed from England. He hoped to sail to Japan or China, but instead he discovered a new land. The explorer was John Cabot, and his ship was called the 'Matthew'.

John Cabot was born in Italy in about 1451. His Italian name was Giovanni Caboto. In Italian, 'caboto' means 'a coastal seaman'. It was quite a common name given to sailors and navigators. When he moved to England his Italian name was changed to 'John Cabot'. This is the name we use today.

The 1400s and 1500s were a time of adventure. Sailors went in search of new lands and new routes towards Asia. The most famous explorer was Christopher Columbus. In 1492 he sailed across the Atlantic Ocean, hoping to find a sea route to Asia. He knew that if he succeeded he would return with spices, silk and other valuables. Instead of Asia, he sailed to North America. He landed on the islands of the West Indies. Columbus thought they were part of Asia.

John Cabot knew Columbus. When Columbus told him about the islands he had found, Cabot planned a voyage of his own. He asked the kings of Spain and

▲ John Cabot lived from about 1451 to 1498. His sons Lewis, Sebastian and Santius were also explorers. John Cabot took the English language to North America.

◄ A cannon was fired as the replica 'Matthew' was launched into the water at Bristol in September 1995.

Text and photographs: Courtesy of the 'Matthew' Project, Bristol Illustration: Mark Stacey

▲ The 'Matthew' is 24 metres (78 feet) long. There are three masts, two of which have square sails.

Portugal to help. Just like Columbus, Cabot thought he would find Asia. Cabot promised to bring spices and silks in return for the money he needed to make his voyage possible. But the kings did not help him.

Cabot went to England. He settled in Bristol. King Henry VII and the merchants of Bristol agreed to pay for his voyage. In May 1497, John Cabot and a crew of 18 sailed from Bristol in search of Japan or China. Their little ship was called the 'Matthew'.

On June 24, 1497, Cabot landed in North America. He called it the 'New Founde Landes', which we know today as Newfoundland, Canada. Cabot explored over 900 miles of coastline, sailing down the east coast of North America.

He returned to Bristol on August 5, 1497, where he was greeted as a hero. When the king heard about Cabot's discovery, he paid him £10 and asked him to make a second journey. In May 1498, Cabot set sail with five ships and 200 men. Cabot died during this voyage, and little is known of his second expedition to the 'New Founde Landes'.

The 'Matthew'

1997 is the 500th anniversary of John Cabot's voyage to North America. A full-size replica of 'Matthew' has been built in Bristol. On May 2, 1997, the 'Matthew' will sail from Bristol with a crew of 18. She will follow Cabot's route and will arrive in Canada on June 24, exactly 500 years to the day after Cabot.

The Otter

Otters are intelligent, graceful and secretive animals. Their numbers have gone down, but now people are working to save them.

Colin Carver/RSPCA

Otter facts

The otter is linked to the family of animals that includes martens, minks, stoats and weasels. Its fur is normally chestnut brown with a white belly and face. It eats meat and its young are called cubs. In water it speeds along at 14km/h using its tail and strong webbed feet. On land, although awkward, it can catch birds and frogs.

The type of otter that lives in Europe is one of 13 species of otter worldwide. It can measure up to one metre from nose to tail. Otters are found living in rivers, lakes, streams, marshes and along coasts, from the Arctic Circle to Africa and South America. In Britain they are found mainly in Scotland and north Wales.

Otters, though great swimmers, rarely stay in the water for longer than 30 minutes at a time. They are insulated (kept warm) by a thick layer of fat, covered by fine down and longer oily hair.

Otters are skilled hunters. They eat small birds and mammals, even frogs and crabs, but their favourite food is fish. Sometimes otters are blamed for stealing fish from salmon and trout farms.

Otters in decline

In the past 40 years or so, humans have created more and more problems for the otter. The number of otters has declined by one third. In the past they were hunted for their fur. Today, it is pollution that threatens the otter.

Otters need to be near water (fresh or salt) and have the protection of trees or bushes on nearby banks. The greater use of weed killers, fertilisers and pesticides by farmers has polluted many of the areas where otters used to live. Otters have retreated to more remote areas of Scotland and Wales. Even here, however, the otter is still in danger.

Text: Stephen Nixey

Colin Seddon/RSPCA

Help at hand

What is being done to help the otter? The answer for otter conservation is to expand Britain's nature reserves and provide new ones. Also, we could stop clearing river banks and draining marshland.

There are now areas called 'otter havens', which were first introduced in the Netherlands. Havens are areas of water which are protected and are safe places for otters to live. The Forestry Commission gives otters a free run on all its waters, and the RSPB and National Trust have havens on their land too.

For more information about otters, write to:
The Otter Trust
Earsham
Near Bungay
Suffolk NR35 2AF

Stuart Harrop/RSPCA

Germ Defence

Germs are everywhere, in the air, in our homes, even in our beds! If a lot get into our bodies, they can make us very ill. To protect us from germs, our bodies have ways to stop them getting in. If they do get in, we also have special cells whose job it is to fight and kill them. Here are some of the ways we stop germs entering our bodies.

Skin

Your skin is the first line of defence. It forms a barrier to prevent germs entering your body. If you cut yourself, germs can enter your body, so it is important that you always clean cuts. Your body prevents germs from getting inside you through a cut by forming a scab on the surface of your skin. It is a type of temporary skin that protects your body until new skin has been made. When this is ready, the scab drops off, leaving new skin underneath.

Text: Peter Barker Illustrations: Andy Robb

Mouth

Since your mouth is an easy place for germs to enter, your first line of defence is your saliva (spit). This helps to weaken any germs in your mouth. It washes them down into your stomach where the strong juices that digest your food help to kill them.

Blood

Your blood has special cells in it whose job is to protect the body from any germs that enter. If germs get into your body, white blood cells surround and kill them before they can make you ill.

Nose

Every time you breathe air into your nose, you also breathe in germs. To help prevent these entering your body, your nose is lined with small sticky hairs that trap the germs.

Eyes

Your eyes produce tears to keep them clean and to kill any germs that may be on them.

Ears

Your ears have small, sticky hairs inside them to trap germs. They also produce wax to stop germs from getting into your body.

Preventing illness

You can help your body fight germs by eating good food and keeping clean, fit and healthy. Doctors will also give you injections to prevent illness. When you have an injection, the doctor puts lots of weak germs into your body. Because they are so weak, your blood cells learn how to kill them. They remember this so that they will be ready next time to overpower any similar germs.

Remember This?

Do you think you've got a good memory? Here are two tests to find out what your memory is really like!

Names to faces

Look at these ten faces and names for two minutes. Cover up the names with strips of paper or pens and try to match the right name to the right face. Score out of 10.

Mr Green   **Mr Rogers**   **Mrs Roberts**   **Mrs Wong**   **Mr Brown**

Mrs Litten   **Mr Smith**   **Miss Cole**   **Mr Strong**   **Ms Jones**

Text: Ron Crabb
Illustrations: Andy Robb

Kim's game

Listed here are 20 objects. Find each one in the picture. When you have found them all, close the book. Write down the names of as many objects as you can remember. Time yourself – you have two minutes to do this! When the time is up, check to see how many you remembered.

ashtray
book
bottle
box
candle
cup
lamp
mirror
pencil
pineapple
pipe
plate
ruler
scissors
slippers
telephone
torch
tray
typewriter
window

Knights of Old

In England, 600 to 700 years ago, every person had their place in something called the 'feudal system'. At the top was the King, who ruled over everyone. Under the King came the Barons, who were very wealthy men. The Barons looked after very large areas of land. Most lived in castles. The Barons could not look after all their land, so they gave some to Knights to look after. In return, the Knights gave the Barons 40 days' service every year. The Knights were there to protect the people who lived on the Barons' land.

Armour

There were battles between different Barons to try and take land from each other, so life as a Knight could be violent.

Knights wore armour to protect them from sword blows. They wore three layers of body armour over hose (tights) and a shirt. The first layer was an **aketon**, a quilted knee length coat. On top of this, Knights wore a **coat** of small chain links, called chain mail. This was covered with small solid plates of metal. A fabric **surcoat** was worn over the armour. It had a special pattern so that people could tell who the Knight was.

Text: Ron Crabb Illustrations: Mark Stacey

Coats of arms

So that Knights weren't killed by their own side, they wore a sign to show who they were. It was called a Coat of Arms. Different patterns and signs to show family names were painted on shields.

When families married, they merged their Coats of Arms into one by dividing the shield. When their children were married, they divided again. Heralds, who studied Coats of Arms, understood what the signs meant.

A banquet fit for a Knight

Knights and the people who lived in castles loved to eat! Everyone sat in the banqueting room to eat pheasant, salmon, dates, honeycomb, eels, beef, pies, larks and finches.

The peasants (poor people) ate cheese, bacon and milk for their dinner.

Which would **you** rather have?

Things to do

1 Why not make your own armour, using coats, jackets and cardboard plates?

2 Why not make your own family Coat of Arms? Ask someone in your family where they came from and use something about that place on your Coat of Arms. You could draw a ship if you are near the sea, or a sheep if your family are farmers.

3 Why not make a picnic banquet fit for a Knight, with you and your friends wearing your Knight's armour?

Design a Bike!

**Do you enjoy riding a bike?
Have you ever wished your bike had special features?
Have you ever dreamed of designing your own bike?
Have you ever thought about what your ideal bike would look like?**

Why not enter this year's Cub Scout Annual competition?
You can have fun designing your own bike, and your entry might be the winner.
The prize? A brand-new bike!
Put your thinking cap on, and get designing.
Good luck!

Here's what you have to do to enter…

1. **Design your ideal bike.**
   Think about
   • how you would like it to look
   • how you would ride it
   • any special features it might have

2. **Draw your bike design on a sheet of paper. Add:**
   • colours and decoration
   • labels to explain any special features and their uses
   • a name for your bike!

3. **On the back of the paper write:**
   • your name
   • your address
   • your birth date and age
   • the name of your Cub Scout Pack
   • the titles of the 3 things you like best in this annual

4. **Put your design in an envelope.
   Put on a stamp and send it to:**

> Design a Bike!
> Cub Scout Annual 1997 Competition
> Editorial Department
> The Scout Association
> Baden-Powell House
> Queen's Gate
> London SW7 5JS

Entries must arrive on or before 31 January 1997.

Text: Brenda Apsley

The Prize

A super **Raleigh Action Bike** is the great prize on offer for the Cub Scout who comes up with the best bike design!

ALIEN QUEST is the name of this great prize bike. It has been specially designed to look great, and to handle well to give riders a fun, safe ride.

The Raleigh **ALIEN QUEST** Action Bike has lots of special features including:
- ☞ Shimano 5-speed index gearing
- ☞ tough BMX fork for great riding performance
- ☞ computer-game style graphics with Amazon Vapour finish
- ☞ maximum-gloss paint finish
- ☞ straight handlebar with bar ends

Now that you've seen the great prize on offer in this year's Cub Scout Annual competition, what are you waiting for? Get started on your bike design right now!

Please note: the colour specification is subject to change.

Don't forget!

The closing date for entries is **Friday 31 January 1997** and entries will be judged on Monday 3 February 1997. The winner will be notified by post. Sorry – The Scout Association cannot return designs.

The publishers reserve the right to substitute a prize of equal value.

Lots of Laughs

What do you get if you cross a millipede with a parrot?
A walkie-talkie!

Akela: Cubs, I want you to work as hard as ants.
Cub: Do ants work hard **all** the time?
Akela: Yes, they never stop working.
Cub: Then how do they always find time to come to Camp with us?

Uncle: How old are you, Chris?
Chris: Seven.
Uncle: And what are you going to be?
Chris: Eight…

Knock, knock.
Who's there?
Cock-a-doodle.
Cock-a-doodle who?
Who let that chicken in here?

What are hippies?
The bits at the top of your leggies!

Dad: What's your favourite time at school?
Son: Hometime!

Why is rugby like bread?
Because it has scrums…

Mum: Joe, did you eat all those buns?
Joe: I didn't touch one.
Mum: But there's only one left!
Joe: That's the one I didn't touch…

Why is it hard to play a joke on a snake?
You can't pull his leg!

What did the Martian say to the petrol pump?
Take your finger out of your ear when I'm talking to you!

Mum: Eat your peas. They'll put colour in your cheeks.
Joe: But I don't want green cheeks, Mum.

When is the number seven an even number?
When you take the letter 's' away!

Text: Brenda Apsley